MORE THAN A GAME

RESPECT
ON THE COURT

AND OTHER
BASKETBALL SKILLS

by Matt Scheff

CAPSTONE PRESS
a capstone imprint

Published by Capstone Press, an imprint of Capstone.
1710 Roe Crest Drive
North Mankato, Minnesota 56003
capstonepub.com

SPORTS ILLUSTRATED KIDS is a trademark of ABG-SI LLC. Used with permission.

Library of Congress Cataloging-in-Publication Data
Names: Scheff, Matt, author.
Title: Respect on the court : and other basketball skills / by Matt Scheff.
Description: North Mankato, Minnesota : Capstone Captivate is published by Capstone Press, [2021] | Series: Sports Illustrated Kids: More than a game | Includes bibliographical references and index. | Audience: Ages 8–11 years | Audience: Grades 4–6 | Summary: "Being a great athlete takes more than just winning every game. Today's basketball superstars know it takes talent, skill, and respect to make them great. This Sports Illustrated Kids title combines fast-paced action, famous plays, and SEL skills to show what sets your favorite athletes and teams apart-on and off the court"—Provided by publisher.
Identifiers: LCCN 2021002736 (print) | LCCN 2021002737 (ebook) | ISBN 9781663906755 (hardcover) | ISBN 9781663920638 (paperback) | ISBN 9781663906724 (PDF) | ISBN 9781663906748 (Kindle edition)
Subjects: LCSH: Baskeball—Juvenile literature. | Basketball—Training—Juvenile literature. | Basketball for children—Juvenile literature.
Classification: LCC GV885.1 .S336 2021 (print) | LCC GV885.1 (ebook) | DDC 796.323—dc23
LC record available at https://lccn.loc.gov/2021002736
LC ebook record available at https://lccn.loc.gov/2021002737

Editorial Credits
Editor: Alison Deering; Designer: Heidi Thompson; Media Researcher: Morgan Walters; Production Specialist: Tori Abraham

Image Credits
AP Photo: Mark J. Terrill, 28, Pat Sullivan, left Cover, 13, Phelan M. Ebenhack, 26, 27, 29; Getty Images: Andrew D. Bernstein, 7, JC Olivera, 25; iStockphoto: FatCamera, top right Cover, LordHenriVoton, bottom right Cover, xavierarnau, middle right Cover; Newscom: Patrick Gorski/Cal Sport Media, 9, Tcott Winters/Icon Sportswire DGM, 14, Thomas Mcewen/Cal Sport Media, 16, Todd Pierson/EFE, 6, Todd Pierson/Philipp H lsmann, 23, Torrey Purvey/Icon Sportswire DGX, 10, Zach Bolinger/Icon Sportswire DAL, 17; Shutterstock: Avector, (dots) design element, EFKS, (area) Cover, 1, ESB Professional, 24, Jacob Crook - JBC Studios, 5, TandemBranding, 4; Sports Illustrated: Bill Frakes, 21, Bob Rosato, 18, Heinz Kluetmeier, 20, John W. McDonough, 19, Robert Beck, 22

All internet sites appearing in back matter were available and accurate when this book was sent to press.

TABLE OF CONTENTS

Glossary terms are **BOLD** on first use.

BEYOND THE COURT

For many fans, basketball is all about tough defense, towering rebounds, and clutch shots. But the action on the court only tells part of the story. Wins, losses, and **statistics** are important. But many players believe that how they play—and how they treat their opponents— is just as important.

Players from the Sydney Kings and Perth Wildcats shook hands before a 2019 game.

Sportsmanship, character, and respect tell a lot about a player or a team. Players congratulate their opponents after big wins. They applaud other players' **milestones**. They exchange handshakes, hugs, and even jerseys. These are the moments that go beyond the stat sheet and show that respect on the court helps make everyone a winner.

A SHOW OF RESPECT

Players give their all on the court. They battle to
outplay their opponents. Sometimes clashes get heated.
But respecting an opponent is part of being a good sport.

Denver Nuggets guard Jamal Murray fends off
opponent Donovan Mitchell of the Utah Jazz.

Murray talked to Mitchell following the round one game seven of the 2020 NBA playoffs.

Shooting Stars

The 2020 National Basketball Association (NBA) playoff series between the Denver Nuggets and Utah Jazz was a great example. Denver guard Jamal Murray and Utah guard Donovan Mitchell each helped carry their teams to a final, winner-take-all game seven.

In the final seconds of the game, Denver led by two points. Utah's Mike Conley launched a final three-point shot. The ball circled the rim and spun out. Denver had won.

Mitchell fell onto the court. He was exhausted and disappointed. Murray didn't start celebrating. Instead, he helped Mitchell up. The two stars hugged as Murray congratulated Mitchell on a great series. It was a show of respect for a well-played series.

Hitting a Milestone

The final seconds of the season were ticking away in a 2015 game between the Villanova University Wildcats and the West Virginia Mountaineers. Villanova guard Emily Leer's college career was almost over. She sat at 999 career points.

West Virginia coach Mike Carey knew that 1,000 points was a huge milestone for any college player. So, with less than eight seconds remaining in the game, Carey gave the Mountaineers an unusual instruction. Foul Leer so she could go to the free-throw line. That's what they did.

Leer stepped to the line and knocked down one of her two free throws. The basket gave her 1,000 career points. West Virginia went on to win the game. But more importantly, they earned the respect of sports fans everywhere.

9

Oklahoma fans showed their support for player Buddy Hield during a 2016 game against Kansas.

Love from the Fans

Rivalries are a big part of college sports. And fans aren't always kind to opposing players. But in a January 2016 matchup, the University of Oklahoma Sooners and the University of Kansas Jayhawks proved that doesn't always have to be the case.

Oklahoma's Buddy Hield was winding up an amazing college career. He scored a remarkable 46 points in the game. His sharp shooting helped force the game into triple overtime. But Kansas held on for a thrilling 109–106 victory.

A dejected Hield remained on the court after the game to do a TV interview. That's when the Kansas fans surprised him with a loud **ovation**. Hield shared the love. He briefly visited with the Kansas fans and signed autographs before he headed to the locker room.

The exchange proved that it's possible to rise above rivalry and share some respect on—and off—the court.

What Is Sportsmanship?

There are lots of ways to define sportsmanship. Here's how legendary University of Connecticut women's basketball coach Geno Auriemma described it. "It's simple," he said. "It's about being kind and considerate and aware of people's feelings. It comes from knowing that you're occupying a small space in this basketball environment—you're not the center of the universe."

Coming Together

The 1999 Women's National Basketball Association (WNBA) season was tough for the Houston Comets. They had won the league title in 1997 and 1998. But in early 1999, tragedy struck. Point guard Kim Perrot was diagnosed with lung cancer.

The team began their season as Perrot battled the disease. But the cancer had spread. At an emotional game against Utah on August 16, 1999, Perrot's close friend Cynthia Cooper scored 42 points. The fans in the stands responded. In the final seconds, they chanted, "We love you, Kim." Everyone was focused on Perrot and her family.

Perrot passed away a few days later. She was 32 years old. The Comets carried on, supporting each other as a team. They dedicated their third straight league title to Perrot. The team also retired her number 10 jersey, making Perrot the first player in league history to have her jersey retired.

Kim Perrot and her teammates in 1999

Well Wishes

Auburn University's Chuma Okeke was on fire in his team's 2019 National Collegiate Athletic Association (NCAA) tournament game against North Carolina. Okeke was leading his team with 20 points and 11 rebounds in the second half.

Chuma Okeke fell to the court following a knee injury during a 2019 playoff game.

With the ball in his hands, Okeke attacked the rim, looking for more. But as he drove, Okeke's knee buckled. He fell to the floor in pain. Trainers rushed onto the court to treat the injury.

Okeke was helped off the court to get X-rays on his knee. As he left, North Carolina's players lined up to offer their encouragement and appreciation. They knew Okeke was hurting and afraid, and they wanted to lend their support. It was a show of **empathy** that every player and fan could appreciate.

Extending a Hand

Basketball can be a rough sport. Bodies hit the floor as players jump, twist, and scramble for the ball. One of the game's traditions is to help an opponent after he or she has fallen. At almost every level, players know to extend a friendly hand and give a fellow player a little bit of help. It's a great example of social awareness and relationship skills.

PAYING TRIBUTE

Respect on the court often goes beyond the game. Players sometimes use their platform to pay **tribute** to icons, those who have passed on, and social causes. It's a way to show that the game is bigger than just points and rebounds.

Tyler Trent at a 2018 football game between the Purdue Boilermakers and the Auburn Tigers

A Fallen Fan

In 2019, former Purdue University student Tyler Trent lost his fight with cancer at just 20 years old. Trent was a huge fan of his school's teams, the Purdue Boilermakers.

In a display of empathy, the Boilermakers basketball team decided to honor Trent. During warm-ups before their game against Wisconsin on January 24, 2020, they wore T-shirts that read *Hammer Down Cancer*.

The team later sold the shirts to raise money for cancer research. The gesture demonstrated empathy and a sense of community purpose. Then Purdue capped off the night by winning the game 70–51.

Kobe's Farewell

In 2016, Kobe Bryant was finishing up an amazing career as one of the NBA's all-time greats. Bryant had a reputation of being ruthless and focused on the court. But that changed as he played in opposing cities for the last time.

Leading up to his retirement, Bryant visited with opposing players and fans. He signed basketballs, shoes, and just about anything else for his opponents. It was a show of gratitude to basketball fans for everything they had given him.

Bryant celebrated with his daughter Gianna following a 2009 NBA Finals game.

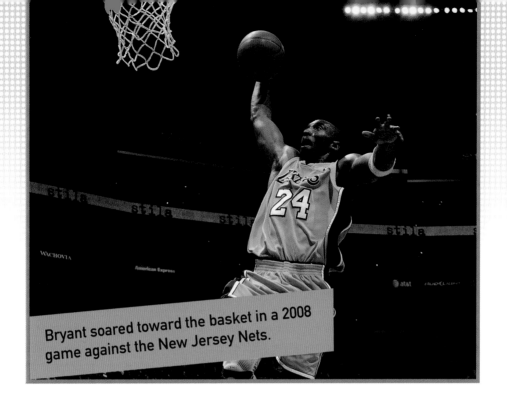

Bryant soared toward the basket in a 2008 game against the New Jersey Nets.

Almost four years later, on January 26, 2020, Bryant, his daughter Gianna, and seven others died in a helicopter crash. People around the world were crushed. Many players—men and women, professionals and amateurs—changed their jersey numbers to 8 or 24, Bryant's former numbers, to honor the fallen superstar.

Honorary Draftee

Gianna Bryant was a rising star in youth basketball when she was killed in a January 2020 helicopter crash. Two of Gianna's teammates from the Mamba Sports Academy basketball team, which was coached by her father, Kobe Bryant, also died in the crash. That April, the WNBA paid tribute, naming Gianna and her teammates—Alyssa Altobelli and Payton Chester—honorary draft picks in the 2020 WNBA draft.

Remembering a Legend

Pat Summit was a college coaching legend. She led the University of Tennessee women's basketball team to eight national championships during a career that spanned almost four decades. Many of her former players took it hard when she died in 2016.

Candace Parker was one of them. Later in 2016, Parker led the Los Angeles Sparks to a nail-biting victory over the Minnesota Lynx in the WNBA Finals.

Head coach Pat Summit on the sidelines in 1989

Candace Parker (left) and Summit (right) during a 2006 game against North Carolina

After her team's 77–76 victory, Parker tried to give an interview. But she was overcome by emotion. All she could say was, "This is for Pat." It was a moving tribute and show of respect to one of the game's greats.

One Last Ovation

In 2019, NBA legend Dirk Nowitzki was playing his final season. Nowitzki was the NBA's first true European-born superstar. His career paved the way for a **generation** of European-born players in the NBA.

The final seconds were ticking away in Nowitzki's last game in Los Angeles against the Clippers. That's when Clippers coach Doc Rivers surprised everyone.

Nowitzki spent his entire NBA career playing for the Dallas Mavericks.

With his team in the lead, Rivers called a time-out, stopping the clock. He grabbed a microphone, called out Nowitzki's name, and urged the crowd to its feet. The crowd quickly joined in, giving the future Hall of Famer one last ovation.

"Honestly, I didn't plan it," Rivers said. "I just felt like he deserved that."

MORE THAN A GAME

Sometimes basketball is about more about wins and losses. It's about overcoming obstacles and changing how people think.

Gettysburg College in Gettysburg, Pennsylvania

One for Weissman

In 2012, Gettysburg College senior Cory Weissman stepped back onto the court. Three years earlier, Weissman had suffered a **stroke** that put his life and career on hold. The stroke—a burst blood vessel in his brain—robbed him of a promising college career. But Weissman fought his way back.

Gettysburg's opponents, Washington College, knew what Weissman had been through. In a show of compassion and sportsmanship, they quickly fouled Weissman, giving him the chance to score.

Both benches stood and cheered as Weissman went to the free-throw line and took his shot. He missed the first. But the second shot was good—earning Weissman the first and only point of his college career.

Cory Weissman in 2012

Remembering Breonna

Social justice was on the minds of WNBA players at the start of the 2020 season, especially following the death of Breonna Taylor. Taylor, a Black woman, was shot and killed in her home by police on March 13, 2020. Her death sparked protests around the country.

WNBA players chose to honor Taylor by dedicating the season to her. In the season's opening game, players from the New York Liberty and the Seattle Storm walked off the court together in a show of **unity**.

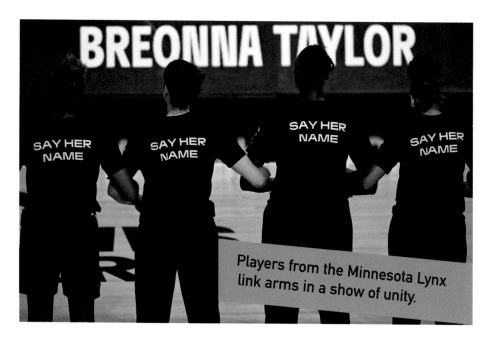

Players from the Minnesota Lynx link arms in a show of unity.

Players from the Phoenix Mercury and the Los Angeles Sparks stand for a moment of silence to honor Breonna Taylor.

When they returned, they spoke about Taylor and social justice. "We will say her name," said Layshia Clarendon of the Liberty. "We will be a voice for the voiceless." Then they held a moment of silence to remember her.

Taking a Stand

Social justice was front and center when the NBA playoffs started in 2020. Police treatment of Black Americans had left many feeling uneasy about race and fairness in the United States.

Many players—Black and white alike—wanted to send a message. In support of social justice, the NBA allowed players to wear messages on their jerseys. Instead of their names, players wore phrases such as Black Lives Matter, Speak Up, and Justice Now.

Kyle Korver of the Milwaukee Bucks displayed the words *Black Lives Matter* on the back of his jersey during a 2020 game against the Miami Heat.

The social justice movement was a major story throughout the 2020 playoffs. The way the NBA and its players handled the issue helped raise discussions about an important issue. They showed that basketball could be far more than just a game.

GLOSSARY

empathy (EM-puh-thee)—imagining how others feel

generation (jen-uh-RAY-shuhn)—a group of people born around the same time

milestone (MILE-stone)—a career achievement, such as scoring 1,000 points

ovation (oh-VEY-shuhn)—a long, loud show of appreciation from a crowd

rivalry (RYE-val-ree)—a fierce feeling of competition between two people or teams

social justice (SOH-shuhl JUHSS-tiss)—the idea that society should treat people of all backgrounds equally and fairly

sportsmanship (SPORTS-muhn-ship)—fair and respectful behavior when playing a sport

statistics (stuh-TISS-tiks)—the science of collecting numerical facts, such as a basketball player's achievements on the court

stroke (STROHK)—a medical condition that occurs when a blocked blood vessel stops oxygen from reaching the brain

tribute (TRIB-yoot)—an action that honors a person or group of people for their accomplishments

unity (YOO-ni-tee)—being together as one

READ MORE

Kortemeier, Todd. *Fairness in Sports*. Lake Elmo, MN: Focus Readers, 2018.

Mattern, Joanne. *What It Takes to Be a Pro Basketball Player*. Mankato, MN: 12-Story Library, 2020.

Robinson, David. *The Ultimate Game: Life Lessons from Sports*. Nampa, ID: Pacific Press Publishing Association, 2019.

INTERNET SITES

10 Basics of Sportsmanship for Kids
verywellfamily.com/basic-sportsmanship-for-kids-1257031

National Basketball Association
nba.com

Women's National Basketball Association
wnba.com

INDEX